The Prodigal Son

Luke 15:1-3, 11-32

Retold by Pamela Broughton
Illustrated by Roberta Collier

A GOLDEN BOOK® • NEW YORK

When Jesus taught, all kinds of people gathered to hear him. Sometimes Jesus ate with the people who gathered.

Some people said, "Jesus does not care who eats with him. He even lets bad people eat at his table."

Jesus heard what they said. This is a story he told to answer them.

There was a rich man who had two sons. He planned to give half his fortune to each son.

One day the younger son said, "Father, give me now
my half of your fortune."

So the man divided all he had between his sons.

The younger son gathered his share together and went away to a far country.

There he wasted all he had. Soon everything was spent.

Then a bad time came to that country, and no one had enough to eat.

The young son began to grow hungry.

So he went out to find work. A man hired him to feed pigs.

No one showed any kindness to the son. He grew so hungry that he would have gladly eaten what the pigs ate.

One day he thought, "Back home, even my father's pig-keeper has more than enough to eat. Yet here I am, dying of hunger."

He said, "I will leave here and go to my father. I will say, 'Father, I have done wrong. I no longer deserve to be your son. But let me work for you.'"

And he rose up and went to his father.

When he was still a long way off, his father saw him.

He kissed his son, and hugged him.

The son said, "Father, I have done wrong. I no longer deserve to be your son."

But the father said to his servants, "Bring the best robe, and put it on him. Put a ring on his finger and shoes on his feet."

He said, "Prepare a great feast, and let us eat and be merry. For my son was lost and now is found again." And they began to be merry.

Now the older son was in the fields. And when he came home, he heard the sounds of music and dancing. He called one of the servants and asked, "What does this music and dancing mean?"

The servant answered, "Your brother has come home safe and sound, so your father has made a feast to celebrate."

The older son was angry and would not join the feast. So his father left the table and begged him to come.

But the brother said, "I have worked for you all these years. I have never disobeyed you. Yet you never made even a small feast for me and my friends.

"But as soon as this bad, wasteful son comes home, you hold a great feast for him."

And the father said to him, "Son, you are always with me. All that I have is yours. But it was right for us to make merry now.

"For your brother was in trouble and now is safe. He was lost and now is found."